EASY PIANO

MY FIRST CHRISTMAS CAROLS SONG BOOK

A TREASURY OF FAVORITE CAROLS TO PLAY

CONTENTS

Cover Painting: *Silent Night*, 1891 by Viggo Johansen
Hirschsprungske Samling, Copenhagen, Denmark / The Bridgeman Art Library

ISBN 978-1-4803-9291-5

HAL•LEONARD®
CORPORATION

7777 W. BLUEMOUND RD. P.O. BOX 13819 MILWAUKEE, WI 53213

In Australia Contact:
Hal Leonard Australia Pty. Ltd.
4 Lentara Court
Cheltenham, Victoria, 3192 Australia
Email: ausadmin@halleonard.com.au

Visit Hal Leonard Online at
www.halleonard.com

Angels We Have Heard on High

Traditional French Carol
Translated by JAMES CHADWICK

Moderately

An - gels we have heard on high sweet - ly sing - ing

o'er the plains, and the moun - tains in re - ply

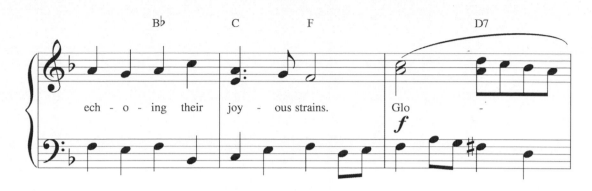

ech - o - ing their joy - ous strains. Glo -

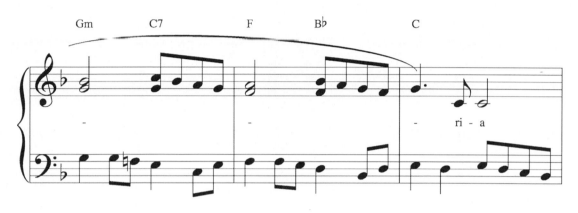

- - - ri - a

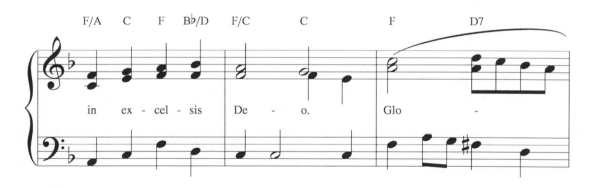

in ex - cel - sis De - o. Glo -

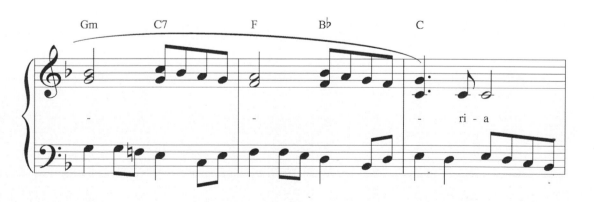

- - - ri - a

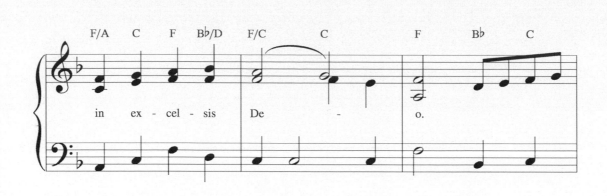

in ex - cel - sis De - o.

Shep - herds why this ju - bi - lee, why your joy - ous

_mf_

strains pro - long? What the glad - some tid - ings be

which in - spire your heav'n - ly song? Glo -

_f_

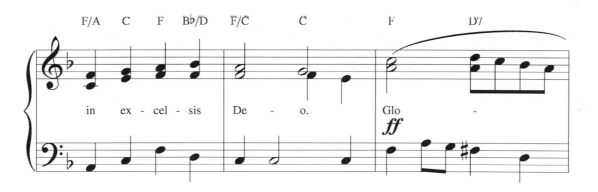

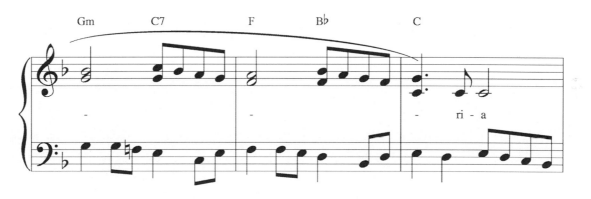

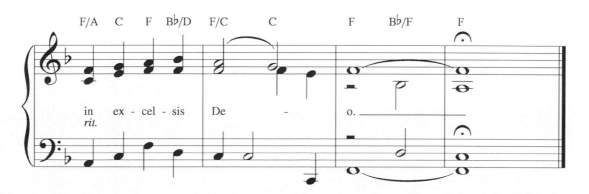

AULD LANG SYNE

Words by ROBERT BURNS
Traditional Scottish Melody

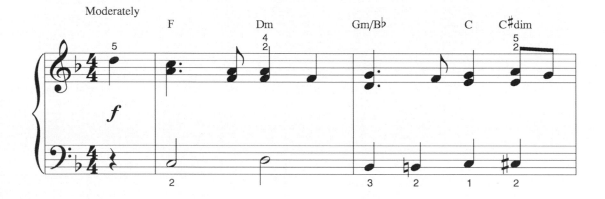

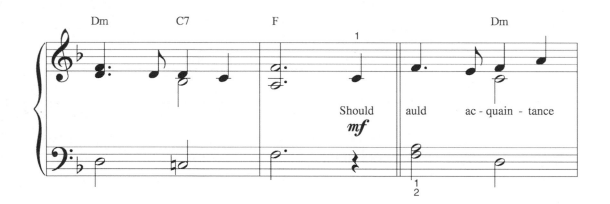

Should auld ac-quain-tance

be for-got and ___ nev-er brought to mind? Should

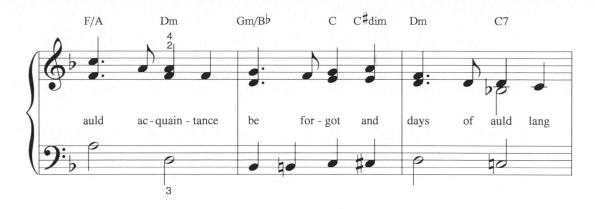

auld   ac-quain-tance   be   for-got   and   days   of   auld   lang

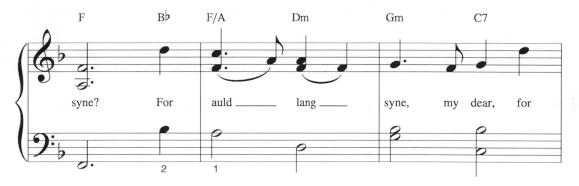

syne?   For   auld   lang   syne,   my dear,   for

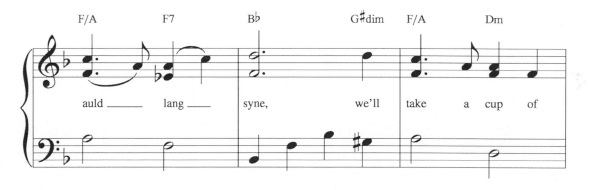

auld   lang   syne,   we'll   take   a   cup   of

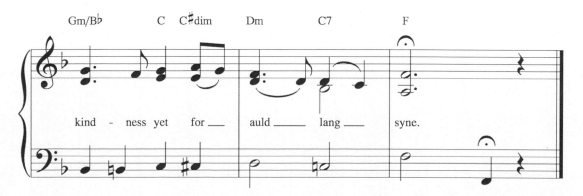

kind-ness yet   for   auld   lang   syne.

Christmas Night (The Blessing of the Oxen), 1902-03, Paul Gauguin

Away in a Manger

Anonymous Text (vv.1,2)
Text by JOHN T. McFARLAND (v.3)
Music by JONATHAN E. SPILLMAN

Tenderly

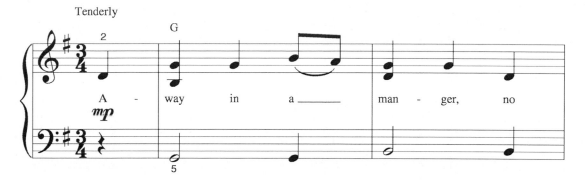

A - way in a _____ man - ger, no

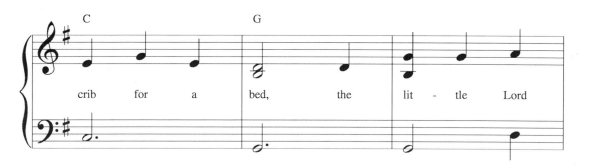

crib for a bed, the lit - tle Lord

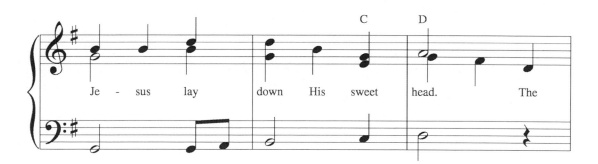

Je - sus lay down His sweet head. The

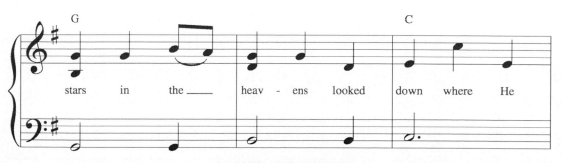

stars in the _____ heav - ens looked down where He

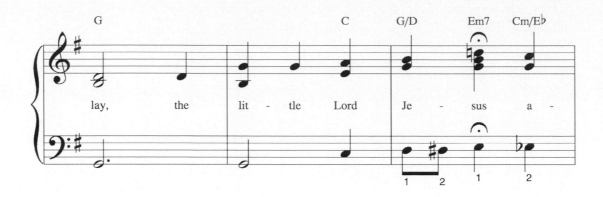

lay, the lit - tle Lord Je - sus a -

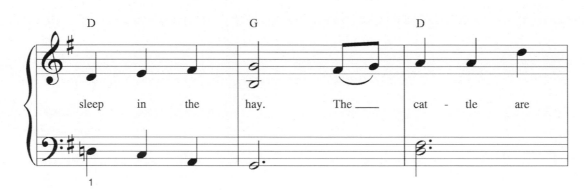

sleep in the hay. The ____ cat - tle are

low - ing; the poor ba - by wakes. But ____

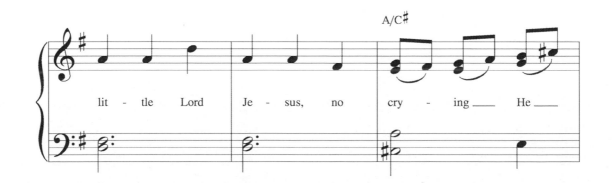

lit - tle Lord Je - sus, no cry - ing ____ He ____

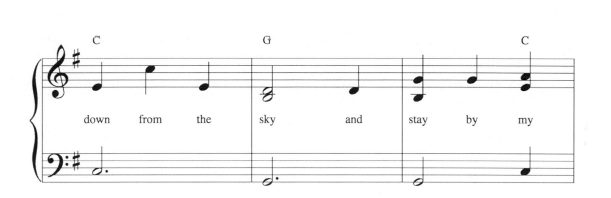

makes.   I love Thee, Lord — Je - sus; look

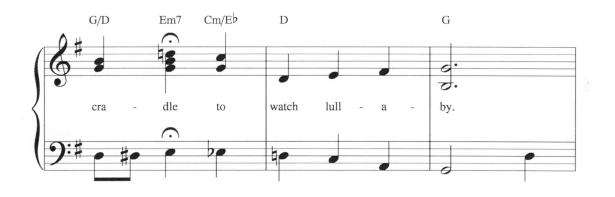

down from the sky and stay by my

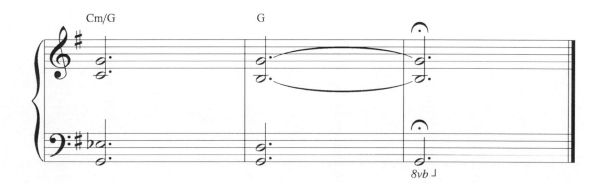

cra - dle to watch lull - a - by.

8vb ⌟

Coventry Carol

Words by ROBERT CROO
Traditional English Melody

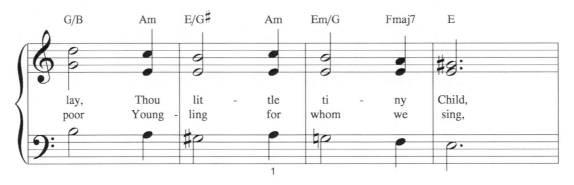

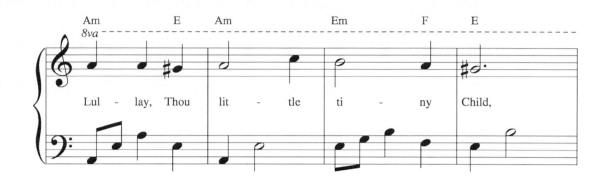

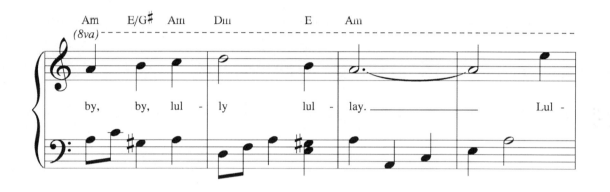

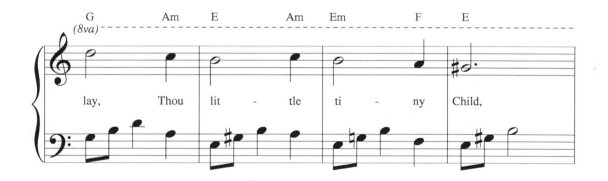

Deck the Hall

Traditional Welsh Carol

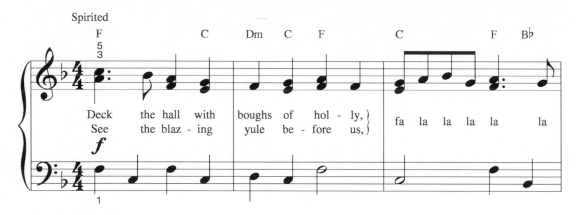

Deck the hall with boughs of hol - ly,
See the blaz - ing yule be - fore us,
fa la la la la la

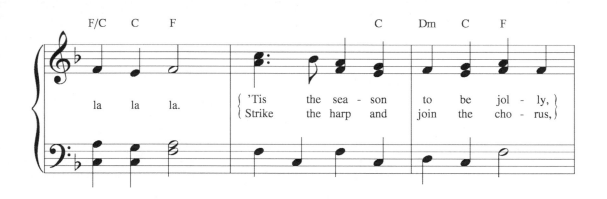

la la la.
'Tis the sea - son to be jol - ly,
Strike the harp and join the cho - rus,

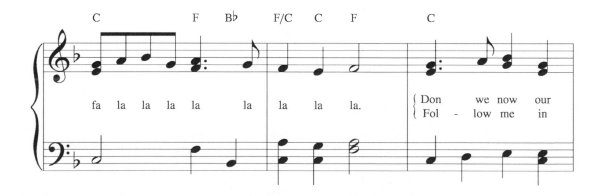

fa la la la la la la la la.
Don we now our
Fol - low me in

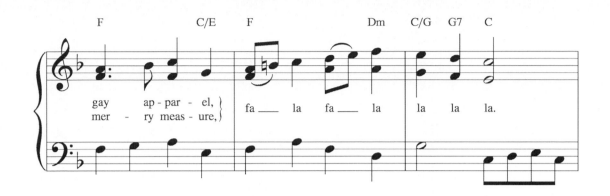

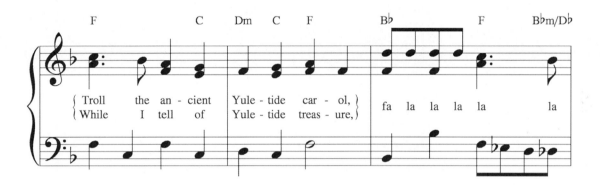

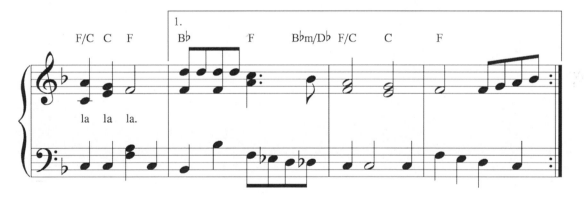

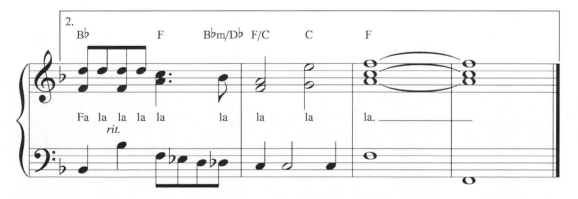

Announcement to the Shepherds, c1600, Manner of Abraham Bloemaert

The First Noël

17th Century English Carol
Music from W. Sandys' *Christmas Carols*

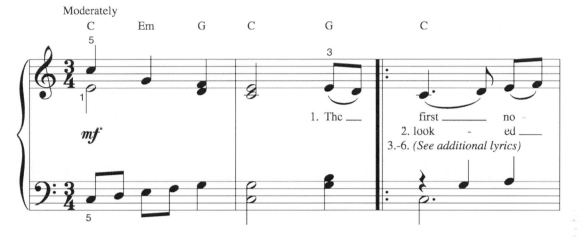

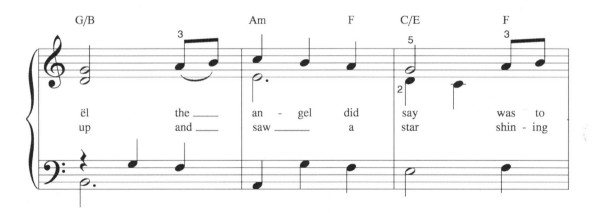

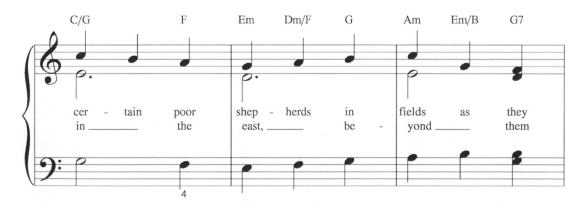

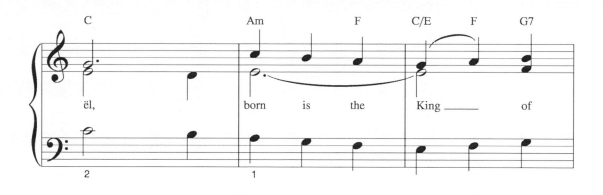

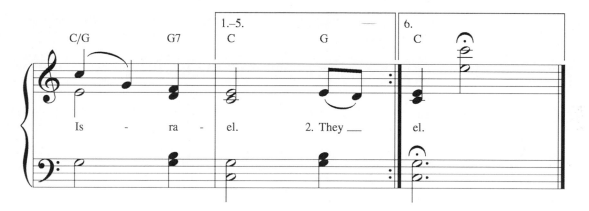

Additional Lyrics

3. And by the light of that same star
   Three wise men came from country far.
   To seek for a King was their intent,
   And to follow the star wherever it went.
   Refrain

4. This star drew nigh to the northwest;
   O'er Bethlehem it took its rest.
   And there it did both stop and stay
   Right over the place where Jesus lay.
   Refrain

5. Then entered in those wise men three
   Full rev'rently upon their knee;
   And offered there in His presence
   Their gold and myrrh and frankincense.
   Refrain

6. Then let us all with one accord
   Sing praises to our heav'nly Lord,
   That had made heav'n and earth of naught,
   And with His blood mankind hath bought.
   Refrain

God Rest Ye Merry, Gentlemen

19th Century English Carol

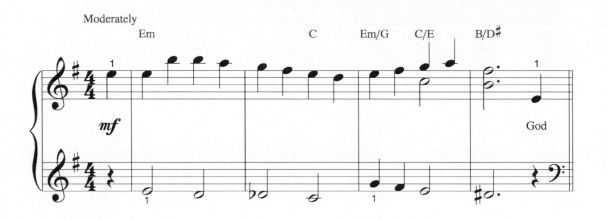

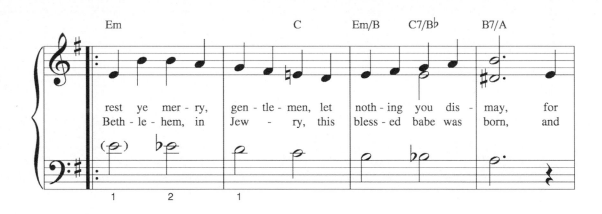

rest ye mer - ry, gen - tle - men, let noth - ing you dis - may, for
Beth - le - hem, in Jew - ry, this bless - ed babe was born, and

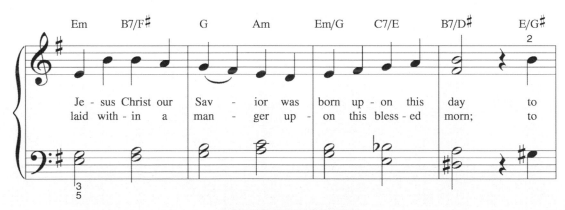

Je - sus Christ our Sav - ior was born up - on this day to
laid with - in a man - ger up - on this bless - ed morn; to

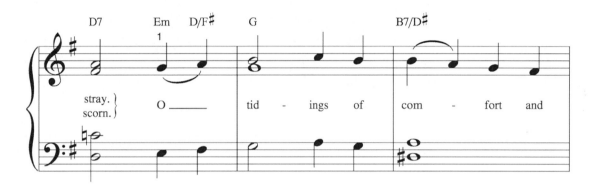

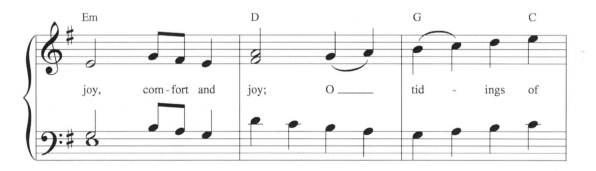

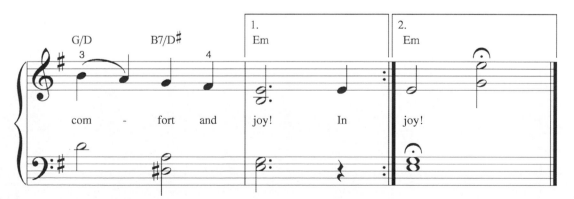

Words by CHARLES WESLEY
Altered by GEORGE WHITEFIELD
Music by FELIX MENDELSSOHN-BARTHOLDY
Arranged by WILLIAM H. CUMMINGS

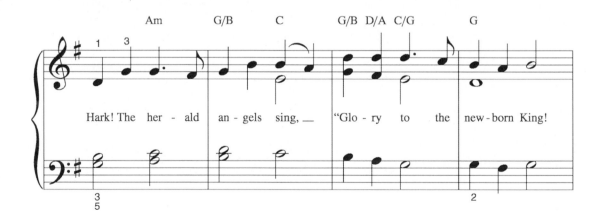

Hark! The her-ald an-gels sing, __ "Glo-ry to the new-born King!

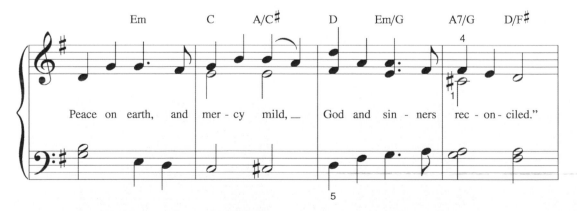

Peace on earth, and mer-cy mild, __ God and sin-ners rec-on-ciled."

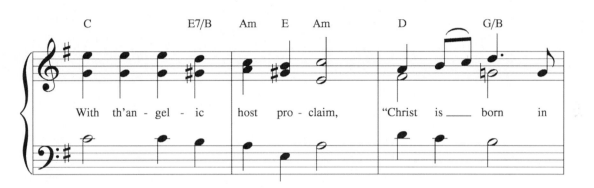

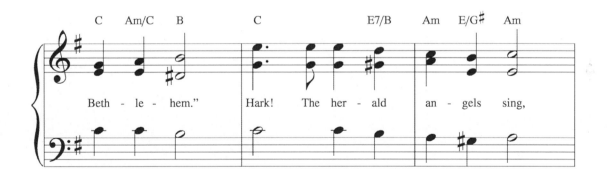

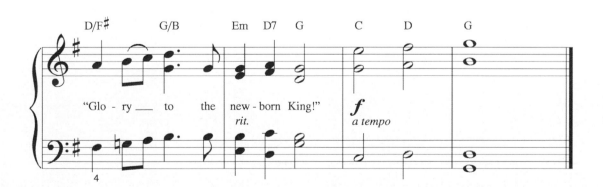

Good King Wenceslas, 1930s, by Treyer Evans / Private Collection / The Bridgeman Art Library

Good King Wenceslas

Words by JOHN M. NEALE
Music from *Piae Cantiones*

Joy to the World

Words by ISAAC WATTS
Music by GEORGE FRIDERIC HANDEL
Adapted by LOWELL MASON

Majestically

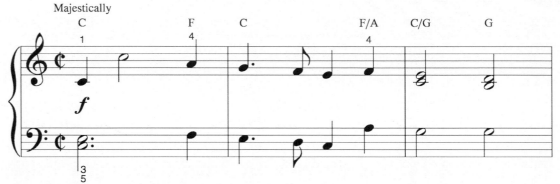

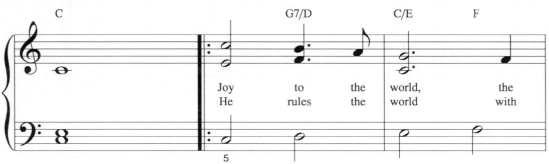

Joy   to   the   world,   the
He   rules   the   world   with

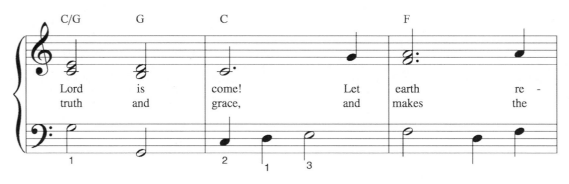

Lord   is   come!   Let   earth   re -
truth   and   grace,   and   makes   the

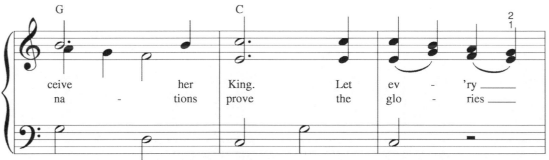

ceive   her   King.   Let   ev -   'ry ____
na -   tions   prove   the   glo -   ries ____

heart _____ pre - pare _____ Him _____ room, _____ and
of _____ His right - eous - ness, _____ and

heav'n and na - ture _____ sing, and _____ heav'n and na - ture _____
won - ders of His _____ love, and _____ won - ders of His _____

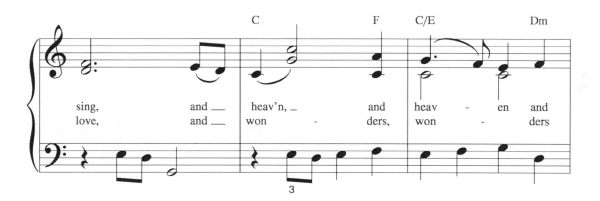

sing, and _____ heav'n, _____ and heav - en and
love, and _____ won - ders, won - ders

na - ture sing.
of His love.

O Christmas Tree

Traditional German Carol

Moderately

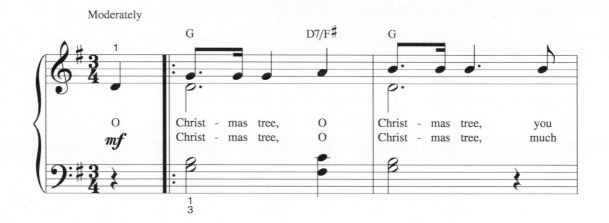

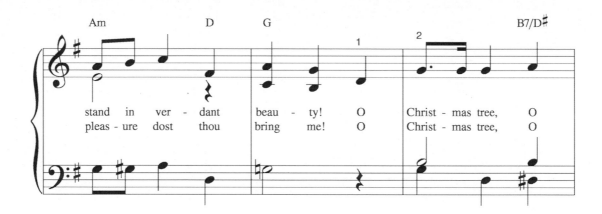

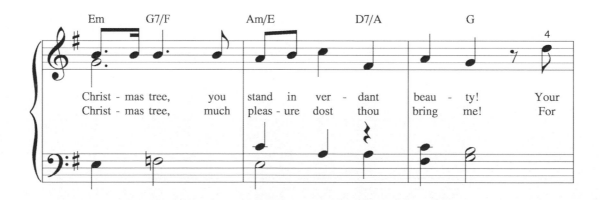

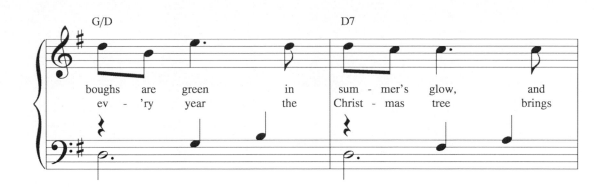

boughs are green in sum - mer's glow, and
ev - 'ry year in the Christ - mas tree brings

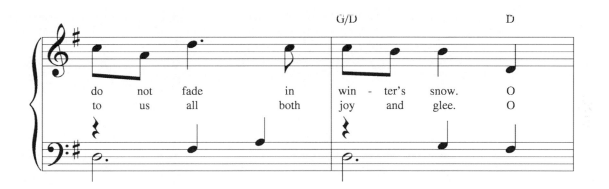

do not fade in win - ter's snow. O
to us all both joy and glee. O

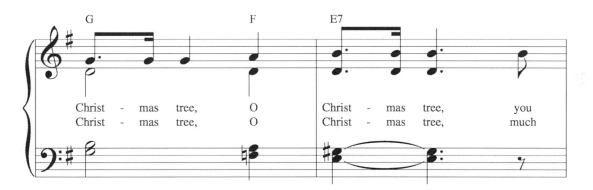

Christ - mas tree, O Christ - mas tree, you
Christ - mas tree, O Christ - mas tree, much

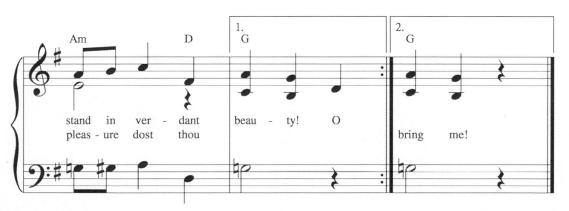

stand in ver - dant beau - ty! O
pleas - ure dost thou bring me!

Christmas Eve, pub. by J. Hoover and Son, 1878 / Private Collection / The Bridgeman Art Library

It Came Upon the Midnight Clear

Words by EDMUND HAMILTON SEARS
Music by RICHARD STORRS WILLIS

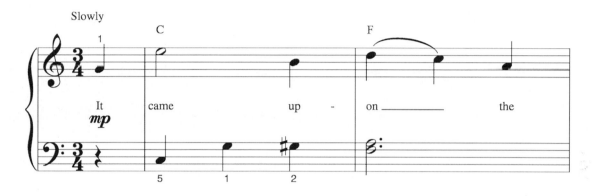

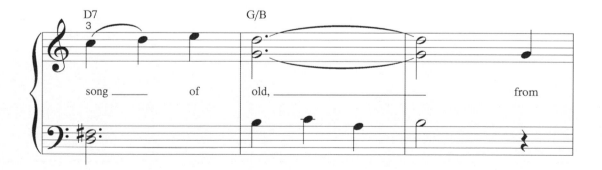

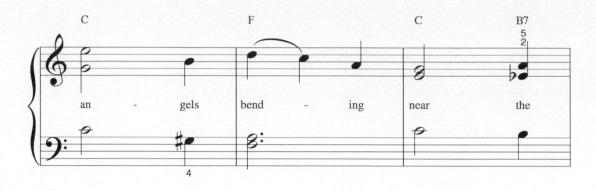

an - gels bend - ing near the

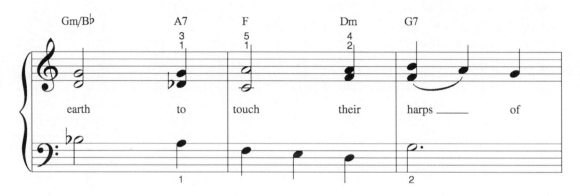

earth to touch their harps ___ of

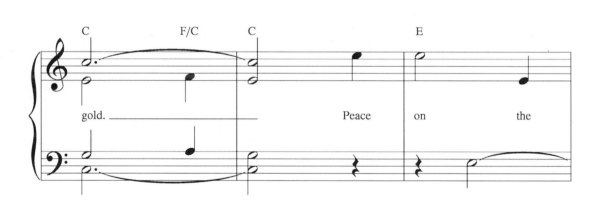

gold. ___ Peace on the

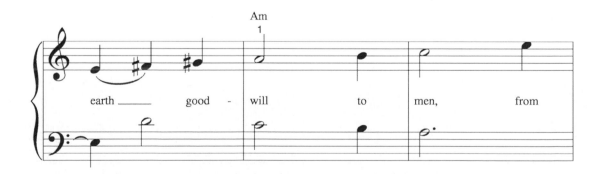

earth ___ good - will to men, from

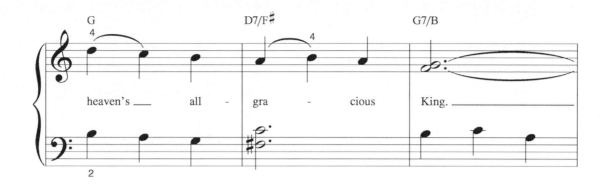

heaven's ___ all - gra - cious King. _____

_____ The world in sol - emn

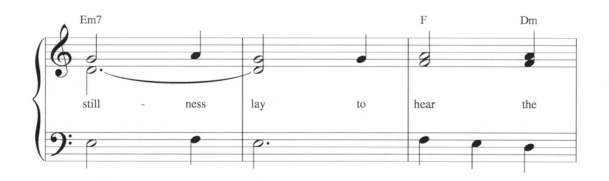

still - ness lay to hear the

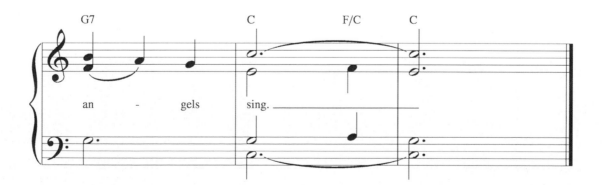

an - gels sing. _____

O Come, All Ye Faithful

Music by JOHN FRANCIS WADE
Latin Words translated by FREDERICK OAKELEY

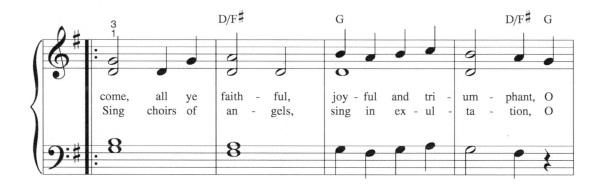

come, all ye faith - ful, joy - ful and tri - um - phant, O
Sing choirs of an - gels, sing in ex - ul - ta - tion, O

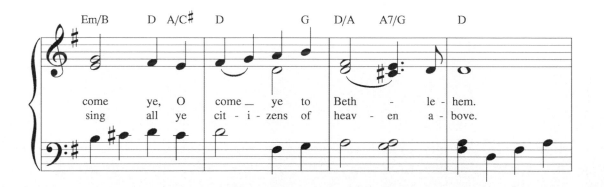

come ye, O come __ ye to Beth - le - hem.
sing all ye cit - i - zens of heav - en a - bove.

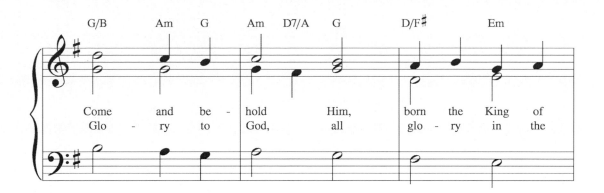

Come and be - hold Him, born the King of
Glo - ry to God, all glo - ry in the

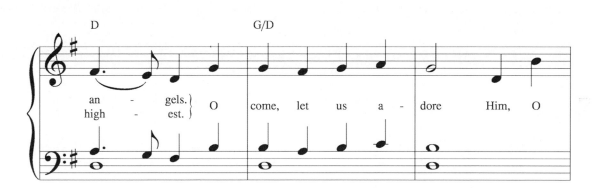

an - gels. } O come, let us a - dore Him, O
high - est. }

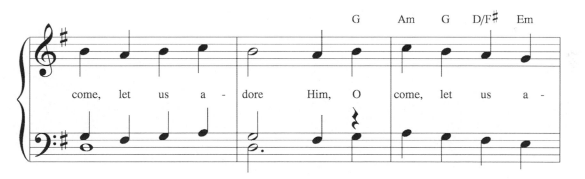

come, let us a - dore Him, O come, let us a -

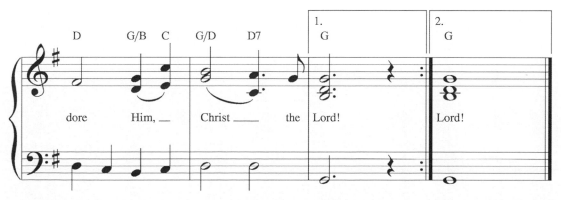

dore Him, __ Christ __ the Lord! Lord!

O HOLY NIGHT

French Words by PLACIDE CAPPEAU
English Words by JOHN S. DWIGHT
Music by ADOLPHE ADAM

O ho - ly
Tru - ly He

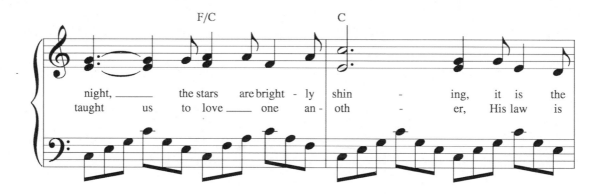

night, _____ the stars are bright - ly shin - ing, it is the
taught us to love _____ one an - oth - er, His law is

night of the dear Sav - ior's birth.
love and his gos - pel is peace.

F/C

Long lay the world ____ in sin and er - ror
Chains shall He break, for the slave ____ is our

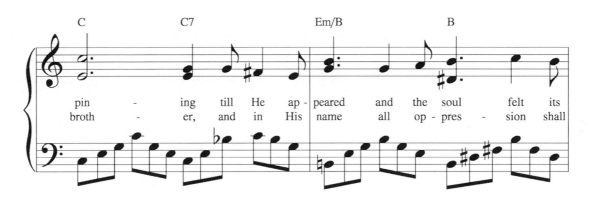

C   C7   Em/B   B

pin - ing till He ap - peared and the soul felt its
broth - er, and in His name all op - pres - sion shall

Em   G7

worth. _____ A thrill of hope, the
cease. _____ Sweet hymns of joy in

C   G7

wea - ry soul re - joic - es, for yon - der breaks a
grate - ful cho - rus raise we, let all with - in us

new   and glo - rious morn.
praise His ho - ly name.

Fall _____ on your
Christ _____ is the

knees, _____ oh
Lord, _____ oh

hear _____ the an - gel
praise _____ His name for-

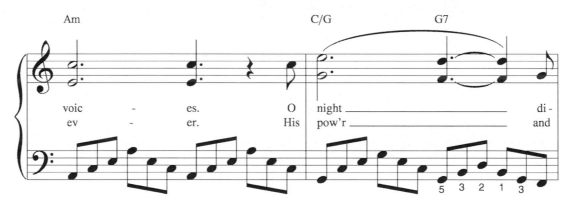

voic - es.   O
ev - er.   His

night _____ di-
pow'r _____ and

vine, _____ O ____
glo - ry ____ ev -

night _____ when Christ was
er - more pro-

born. _____ O night, _____ O
claim. _____ His pow'r _____ and

1.

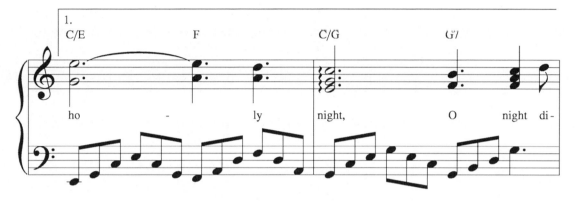

ho - ly night, O night di-

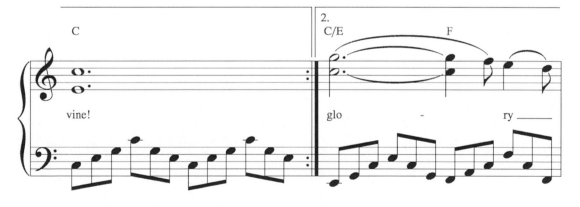

vine!　　　　　　**2.**　glo - ry _____

ev - er - more pro - claim.
rit.

A Christmas Party, 1852, George Henry Durrie

Bells on bob - tail ring, mak - ing spir - its
horse was lean and lank, mis - for - tune seemed his

bright; what fun it is to ride and sing a
lot, —— he got in - to a drift - ed bank and

sleigh - ing song to - night! Oh!)
we, we got up - sot! Oh!) Jin - gle bells,

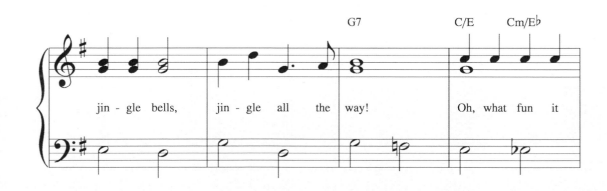

jin - gle bells, jin - gle all the way! Oh, what fun it

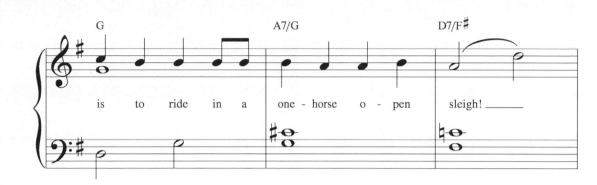

is   to   ride   in   a   one - horse   o - pen   sleigh! ____

Jin - gle   bells,   jin - gle   bells,   jin - gle   all   the

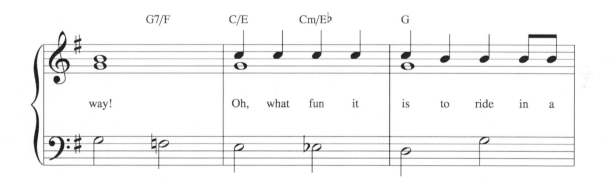

way!   Oh,   what   fun   it   is   to   ride   in   a

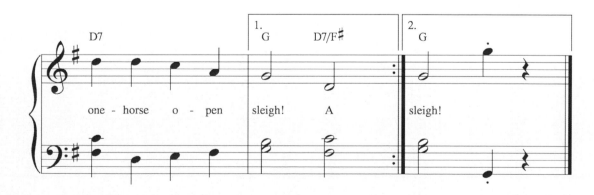

one - horse   o - pen   sleigh!   A   sleigh!

O Little Town of Bethlehem

Words by PHILLIPS BROOKS
Music by LEWIS H. REDNER

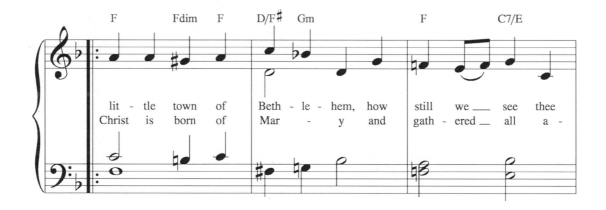

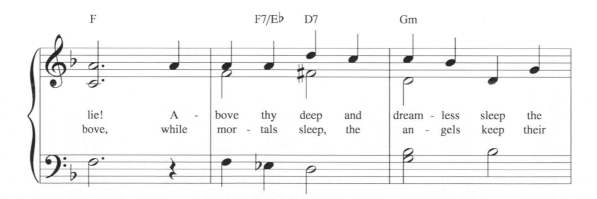

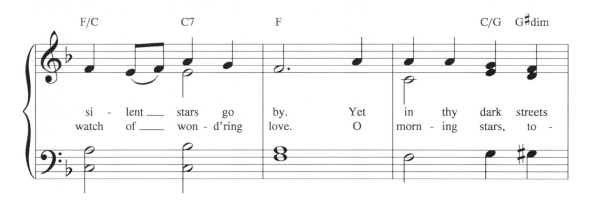

si - lent ___ stars go by. Yet in thy dark streets
watch of ___ won - d'ring love. O morn - ing stars, to -

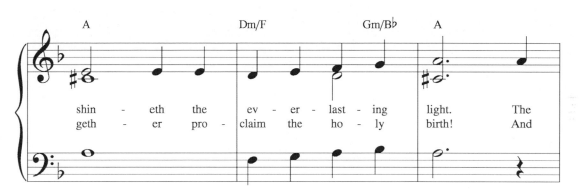

shin - eth the ev - er - last - ing light. The
geth - er pro - claim the ho - ly birth! And

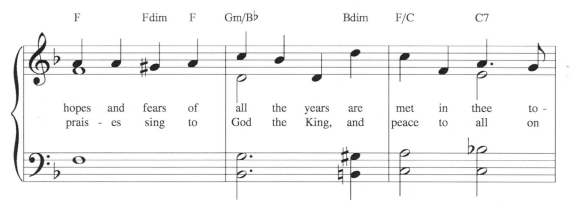

hopes and fears of all the years are met in thee to -
prais - es sing to God the King, and peace to all on

1.
night. For

2.
earth!

Words by JOSEPH MOHR
Translated by JOHN F. YOUNG
Music by FRANZ X. GRUBER

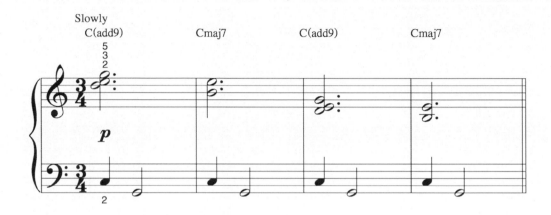

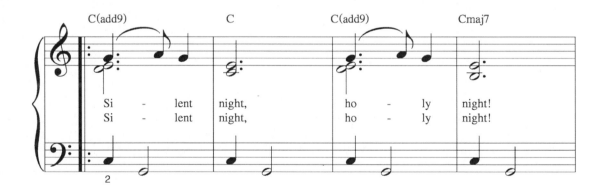

Si - lent night, ho - ly night!
Si - lent night, ho - ly night!

All is calm, all is bright.
Shep - herds quake at the sight.

The Happy Family (panel), Andre Henri Dargelas / © Wolverhampton Art Gallery, West Midlands, UK / The Bridgeman Art Library

March of the Toys

By VICTOR HERBERT

Strict March tempo

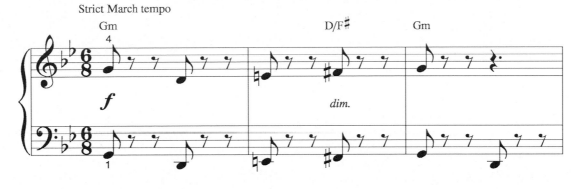

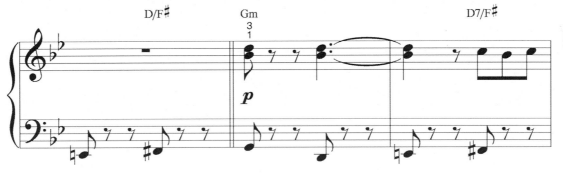

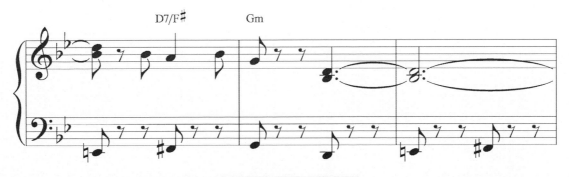

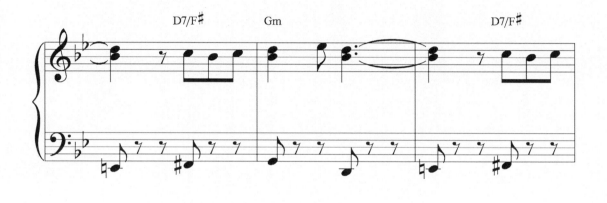

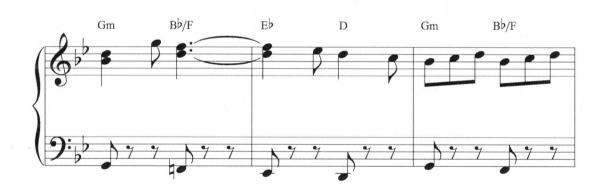

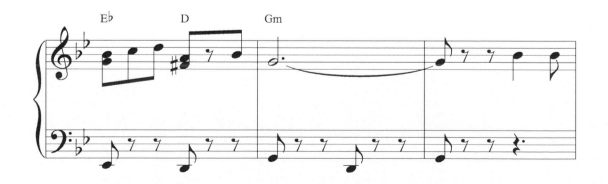

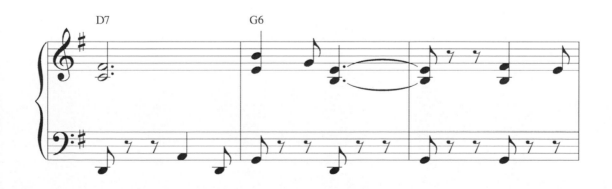

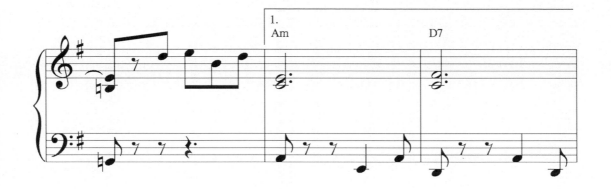

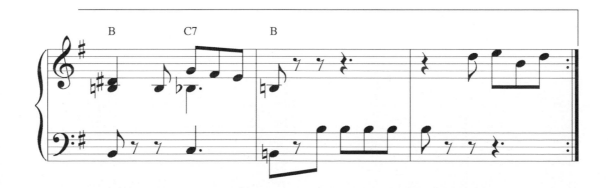

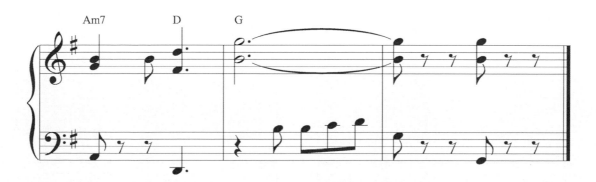

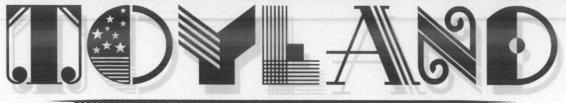

TOYLAND

Words by GLEN MacDONOUGH
Music by VICTOR HERBERT

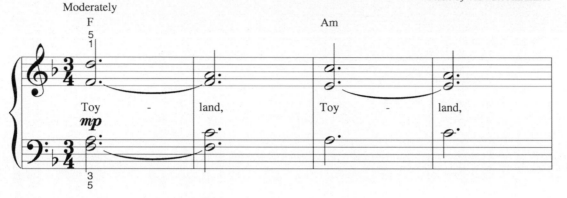

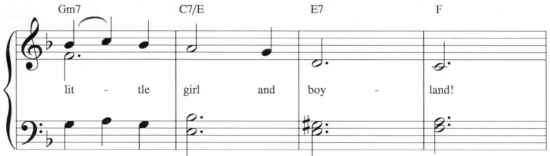

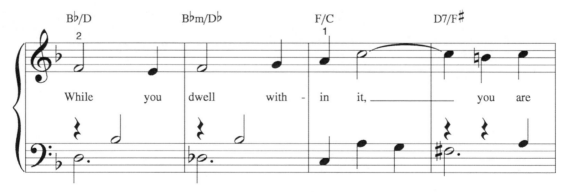

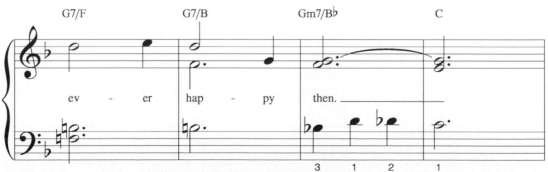

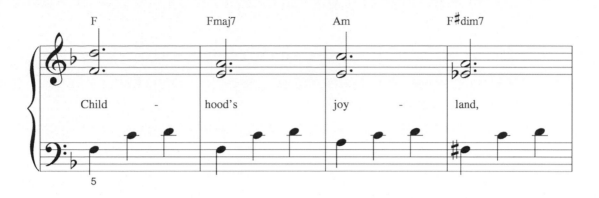

F   Fmaj7   Am   F#dim7

Child — hood's   joy — land,

Gm7   C7/E   E7   F

mys — tic   mer — ry   joy — land,

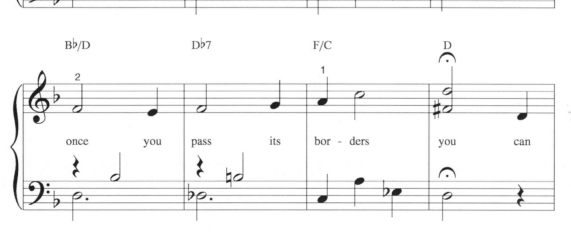

Bb/D   Db7   F/C   D

once   you   pass   its   bor — ders   you   can

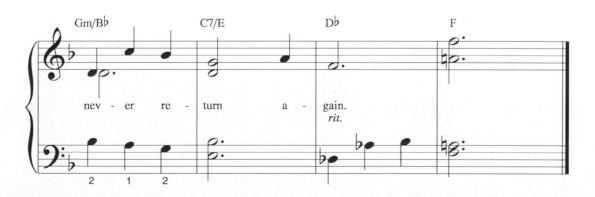

Gm/Bb   C7/E   Db   F

nev — er   re — turn   a — gain.
rit.

THE TWELVE DAYS OF CHRISTMAS

Traditional English Carol

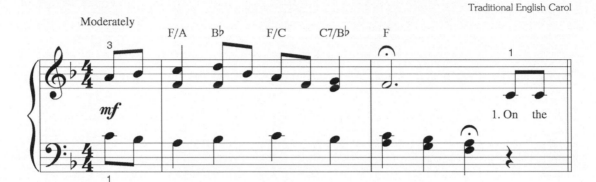

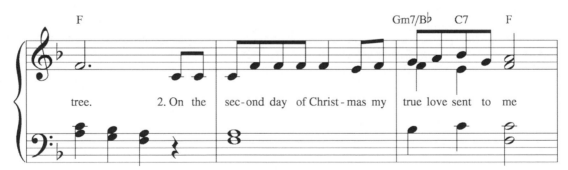

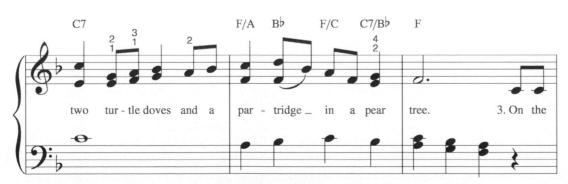

third day of Christ - mas my true love sent to me three French hens,

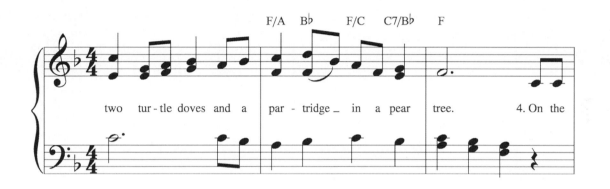

two tur - tle doves and a par - tridge in a pear tree. 4. On the

fourth day of Christ - mas my true love sent to me four call - ing birds,

three French hens, two tur - tle doves and a par - tridge in a pear

tree.   5. On the fifth day of Christ - mas my true love sent to me

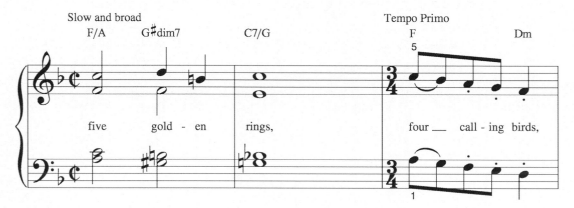

Slow and broad   **Tempo Primo**

five   gold - en   rings,   four ___ call - ing birds,

three French hens,   two ___ tur - tle doves and a   par - tridge ___ in a pear

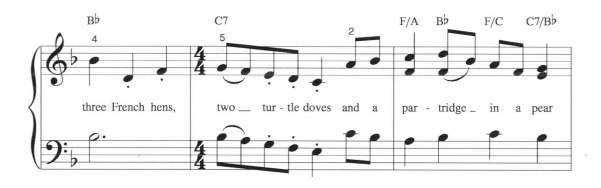

tree.   6. On the sixth day of Christ - mas my true love sent to me
7.-12. *(See additional verses)*

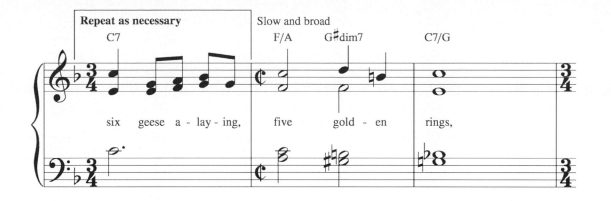

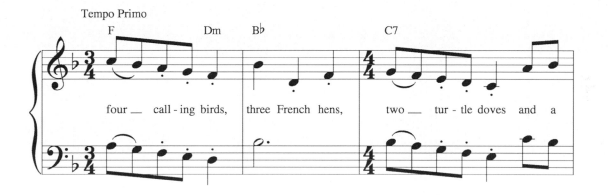

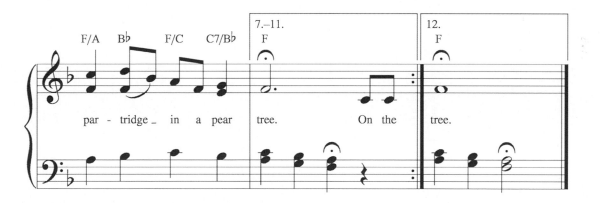

Additional Verses

Seven swans a-swimming
Eight maids a-milking
Nine ladies dancing
Ten lords a-leaping
Eleven pipers piping
Twelve drummers drumming

Santa Coming Down the Chimney, c 1870, artist unknown

Up On the Housetop

Words and Music by
B.R. HANBY

Who would-n't go!   Ho, ho, ho!   Who would-n't go! ____

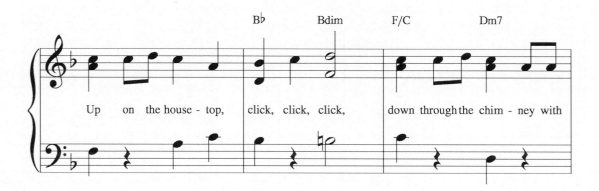

Up on the house-top,   click, click, click,   down through the chim - ney with

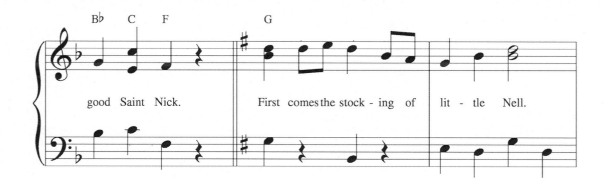

good Saint Nick.   First comes the stock - ing of   lit - tle Nell.

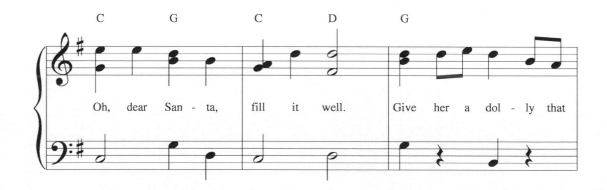

Oh, dear San - ta,   fill it well.   Give her a dol - ly that

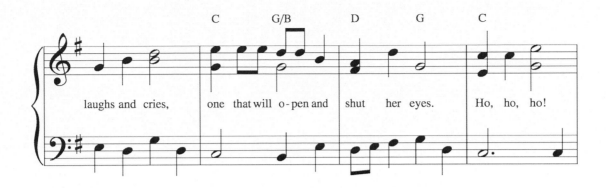

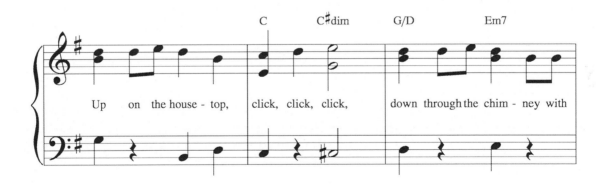

WE THREE KINGS OF ORIENT ARE

Words and Music by
JOHN H. HOPKINS, JR.

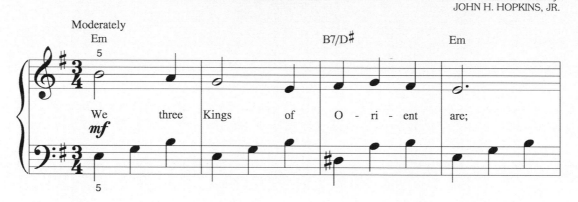

We three Kings of O - ri - ent are;

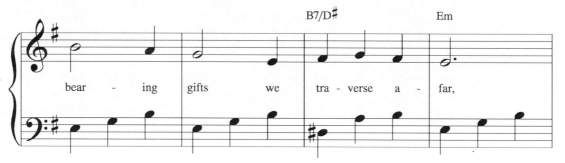

bear - ing gifts we tra - verse a - far,

field and foun - tain, moor and moun - tain,

fol - low - ing yon - der star. O _____

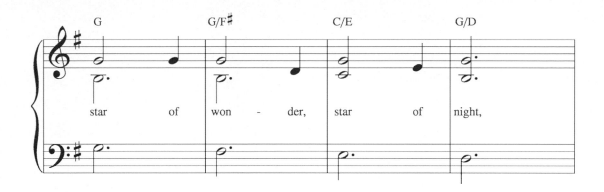

star of won - der, star of night,

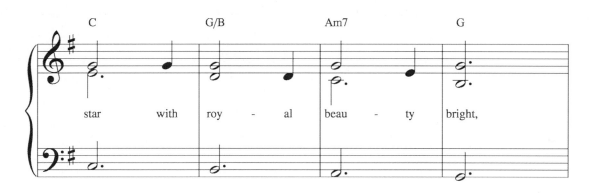

star with roy - al beau - ty bright,

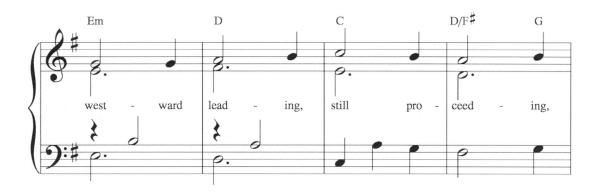

west - ward lead - ing, still pro - ceed - ing,

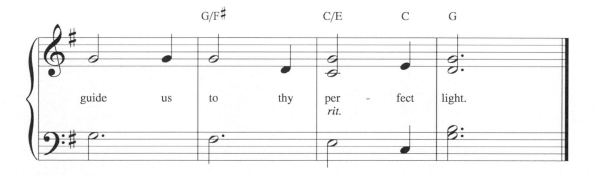

guide us to thy per - fect light.

rit.

We Wish You a Merry Christmas

Traditional English Folksong

We wish you a mer-ry Christ-mas, we wish you a mer-ry

Christ-mas, we wish you a mer-ry Christ-mas, and a hap-py New

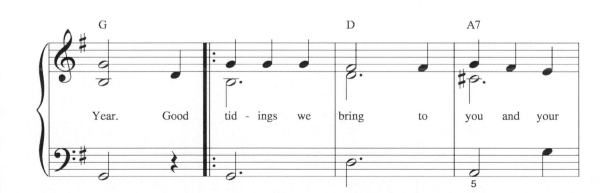

Year. Good tid-ings we bring to you and your

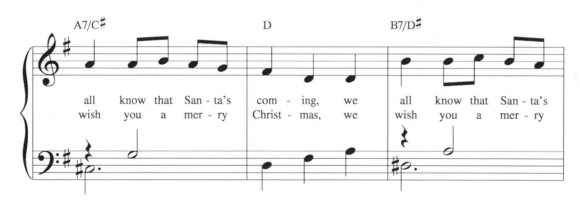

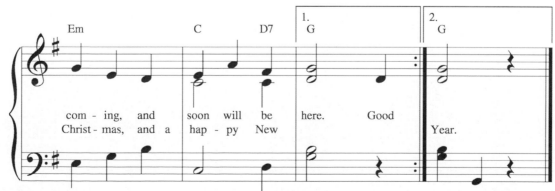

Song of the Angels, 1881, William-Adolphe Bouguereau

What Child Is This?

Words by WILLIAM C. DIX
16th Century English Melody

What child is this, _____ who, laid to

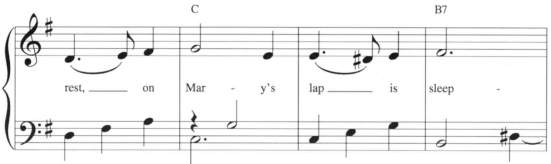

rest, _____ on Mar - y's lap _____ is sleep -

ing? Whom an - gels greet _____ with an - thems

sweet, _____ while shep - herds watch _____ are keep -

ing?   This,   this _____ is   Christ   the

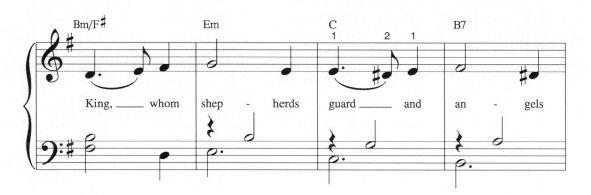

King, _____ whom   shep - herds   guard _____ and   an - gels

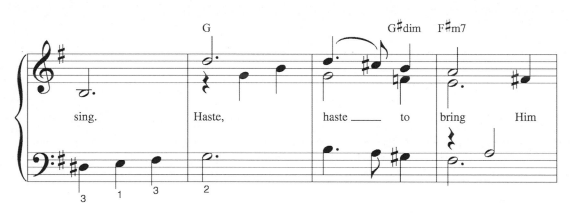

sing.   Haste,   haste _____ to   bring   Him

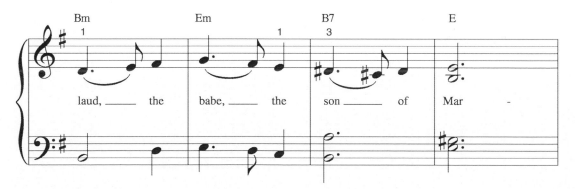

laud, _____ the   babe, _____ the   son _____ of   Mar -

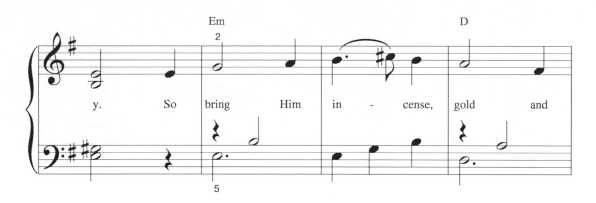

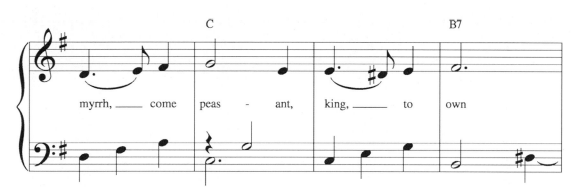

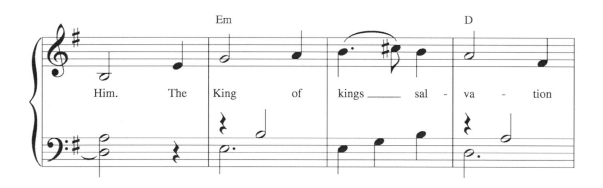

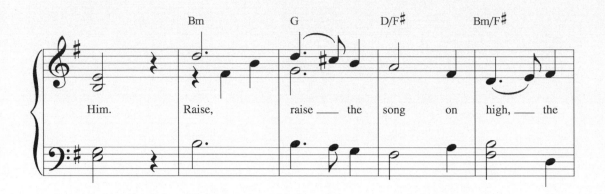

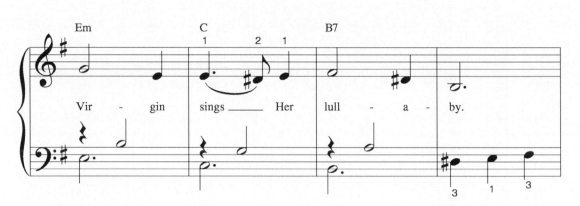